SUMMARY
of

The Subtle Art of Not Giving a F*ck

A Counterintuitive Approach to Living a Good Life by Mark Manson

CompanionReads

Dear readers:

This is an unofficial summary & analysis of Mark Manson's *The Subtle Art of Not Giving a F*ck* designed to enrich your reading experience. Buy the original book here: http://bit.ly/mansonsart

CompanionReads

errors or omissions. Upon using the information contained in this book, you agree to hold harmless the author from and against any damages, costs, and expenses, including any legal fees, potentially resulting from the application of any of the information provided by this guide. The disclaimer applies to any damages or injury caused by the use and application, whether directly or indirectly, of any advice or information presented, whether for breach of contract, tort, neglect, personal injury, criminal intent, or under any other cause of action. You agree to accept all risks of using the information presented inside this book.

The fact that an individual or organization is referred to in this document as a citation or source of information does not imply that the author or publisher endorses the information that the individual or organization provided. This is an unofficial summary and analytical review and has not been approved by the original author of the book.

Attention: Our FREE Gift to You

As a way to say "Thank You" for being a fan of our series, we've included a free gift for you:

Get Our How to Learn More Effectively Video Playlist...

for you, free.

If you'd like one, please visit:

http://www.companionreads.com/gift

The CompanionReads Team

Table of Contents

Book Abstract of Mark Manson's *The Subtle Art of Not Giving a F*ck*

Self-help books abound, but most of them will leave you feeling more worthless or confused than before. Not so with *The Subtle Art of Not Giving a F*ck*. This self-help guide cuts through the fatty excess of most advice to show you why it's okay to not think positively all the time. In fact, it will teach you to stop caring about everything so much.

While you've been told for decades that opening yourself up to ideas and thinking happy thoughts is the key to wealth and happiness, Mark Manson is ready to send you a different message. He believes that caring about everything is worse than caring about nothing, and the key to a fulfilling life is carefully deciding exactly what you will direct your attention towards.

In this irreverent, often hilarious recounting of his own life's foibles, Mark teaches you what it takes to accept the inevitable problems that come with life and how to keep living beyond your limitations.

Chapter Summary of Mark Manson's
*The Subtle Art of Not Giving a F*ck*

Chapter 1: Don't Try

Main Idea:

The American dream is to keep trying until something succeeds. As a culture, we celebrate success stories where people overcome all odds to achieve great things. However, there isn't always a formula for success. Sometimes, the best success comes from simply not caring what others think, being unflinchingly honest about where you are, and not dwelling on what you don't already have.

Supporting Ideas:

The Feedback Loop from Hell

The problem with most self-help advice is that it constantly emphasizes what you lack. By setting goals, you begin to fixate on your shortcomings and what you don't have already. Beautiful people don't stand in front of mirrors convincing themselves they're beautiful–they just know it.

In the same way, fixating on what you don't like about your life will only make the negative more apparent. Knowing that you suffer from anxiety in front of crowds will only make you more anxious, and you'll soon feel anxious about feeling anxious (or angry for feeling angry, unloved for feeling unloved, etc.). This negative feedback loop can be overpowering and leaves you feeling neurotic, stressed and self-loathing. The more you want to feel rich, successful or important, the more you will be aware of the ways you aren't.

The Subtle Art of Not Giving a F*ck

Sometimes, the key to starting to feel better about your achievements is to simply not care as much. It's impossible to care about everything that happens in life, and without some restrictions on what you care about, you'll find yourself wasting your valuable energy caring about things that don't matter. According to Manson, the key to a more fulfilling life is prioritizing and focusing your thoughts effectively so that they match your deep-held personal values.

This doesn't mean you become indifferent or apathetic, it means you are confident about feeling different than the majority. Indifferent people tend to be afraid of the making a decision and standing for something, so they let life pass by. In contrast, caring deeply about something inspires action. The people that aren't afraid to stand out and risk failure are the ones that go on to truly succeed.

In contrast, if you find yourself caring too much about things that don't matter, you probably don't have enough in your life to care about. Without a place to direct your energy, you will find yourself blowing up over problems with coworkers or grocery stores not accepting your coupons.

So Mark, What the F*ck is the Point of This Book Anyway?

The point of this book is to help you understand what you're choosing to view as important in your life and why you're choosing it. Society is training us to think that it's not okay for life to be hard sometimes, which is why it's all too easy to care about the wrong things or self-medicate with alcohol, TV and other distractions. No matter what, life will be full of problems and a self-help book isn't going to change that. Instead, it can teach you how to let go of what's unimportant and turn your worst, unwanted problems into slightly better problems instead.

Key Thoughts

"The desire for more positive experience is itself a negative experience. And, paradoxically, the acceptance of one's negative experience is itself a positive experience."

"To not give a f*ck is to stare down life's most terrifying and difficult challenges and still take action."

"I believe that today we're facing a psychological epidemic, one in which people no longer realize it's okay for things to suck sometimes. I know that sounds intellectually lazy on the surface, but I promise you, it's a life/death sort of issue."

Chapter 2 Happiness is a Problem

Main Idea:

It's impossible to set up a life for yourself that doesn't involve suffering. Rich people suffer from taking care of their riches, and poor people suffer because they don't have them. All suffering isn't equal, but some suffering is still unavoidable. Popular culture wants us to think otherwise. Happiness is often shown as something that can be worked for and achieved, so long as you follow the proper steps to find it. However, the premise that solving problems will make you happy is part of the problem, and it's making us miserable.

Supporting Ideas:

The Misadventures of Disappointment Panda

Mark's favorite (self-invented) superhero is Disappointment Panda. His power would be to go door-to-door and tell people the unpleasant truths about themselves. By telling people the things they are most afraid to face in their lives, Disappointment Panda would free them to face their insecurities and become stronger by working through them.

Pain is the body's way of spurring action, so the pain of facing the truth about yourself is often necessary to change for the better. Touching lit stoves teaches you to avoid red hot metal, and accepting why a relationship is falling apart will help you understand what to do differently next time. As society continues to coddle us from feelings of pain, it's becoming harder than ever to experience the healthy doses of pain that inspire change.

Happiness Comes from Solving Problems

The entirety of life is solving problems. Decisions will never prevent problems from happening, they just upgrade your problems to new ones. Nonetheless, happiness comes from constantly solving problems, not avoiding them. Happiness won't come at a magical point in your career or when your bank account reaches seven figures: instead, it comes from constantly solving the right kinds of problems.

Unfortunately, it's hard for many people to address their problems and move towards solving them. These people are often in denial that their problems exist, or play the victim and refuse to accept responsibility for their problems in the first place. Attributing blame or staying in denial provides a quick high, but it doesn't do anything to get to the root of your problem and will leave you miserable in the long run.

Emotions are Overrated

When you strip them down, emotions are simply a feedback mechanism that helps the human species to reproduce slightly better. They are biological responses designed to nudge behavior in beneficial directions. Because of this, allowing them to have rampant control over every part of our lives and decision making processes is a recipe for disaster. Just because something feels good doesn't mean it is good, and relying on your emotions for guidance will leave you miserable once the emotion disappears. Being a victim to the impulses of your emotions puts you at the same mental level as a three-year-old, and prevents you from making the most beneficial choices for the long run.

Choose Your Struggle

Life is always going to be full of problems, but what you have control over are the kinds of problems that you deal with. You have a choice about the kind of pain you want in your life, and what you're willing to struggle for will dictate what you wind up achieving. Do you want to be a CEO? Get ready to put in decades of 60 work weeks to get there. Looking for the perfect body? Hours of physical discomfort and sweating at the gym await you. Finding happiness will always require struggle and solving problems, but you can choose to face those struggles if they will get you where you want to go. Who you are is defined by the things you're willing to struggle for. It's not about willpower, it's about accepting the process and finding joy in the climb.

Key Thoughts

"We suffer for the simple reason that suffering is biologically useful. It is nature's preferred agent for inspiring change... Pain, in all its forms, is our body's most effective means of spurring action."

"An obsession and overinvestment in emotion fails us for the simple reason that emotions never last. Whatever makes us happy today will no longer make us happy tomorrow, because our biology always needs something more."

"The more interesting question is the pain. What is the pain that you want to sustain? That's the hard question that matters, the question that will get you somewhere. It's the question that can change a perspective, a life. It's what makes me, me, and you, you. It's what defines us and separates us and ultimately brings us together."

Chapter 3: You Are Not Special

Main Idea:

In a world of seven billion people, few can be considered exceptional. Nonetheless, most of us feel that we are uniquely skilled and far superior to the rest of humanity. This "high self-esteem" can be delusional and harmful, especially if you haven't done anything worth having sky high self-esteem about. Thinking that you are exceptional is not a good strategy for becoming exceptional, and it often leads to feelings of entitlement. Entitled people are enclosed in a narcissistic bubble and live under the impression that they need to feel good all the time. This causes them to hide from problems and the opportunities for real growth. True self-esteem comes from accepting the negative parts of your personality and problem solving when necessary.

Supporting Ideas:

Things Fall Apart

Sometimes the most traumatic life experiences create the biggest positive changes in the long term. Mark was busted as a teenager for bringing pot to school, and the implications of this behavior (along with his parent's divorce) dramatically affected the rest of his adolescence. He unconsciously accepted the belief that there were problems in his life too big to solve, and it left him feeling miserable and helpless. However, accepting problems as unsolvable is a foolproof way to feel like you are different and unique, and can lead to entitlement. Thinking that you need special treatment because you're pathetic and everyone else is awesome is just as damaging as thinking you are better than everyone else.

The Tyranny of Exceptionalism

Few of us are truly exceptional at anything, and no one is exceptional at everything. Yet, mainstream media drowns us in stories of the exceptional (both good and bad) so that we feel like we are somehow faulty if we are just normal. Some people combat this problem by being a walking disaster. If they can't be amazing for positive things, they reason, might as well be notorious for being terrible.

B-b-b-but, If I'm Not Going to Be Special or Extraordinary, What's the Point?

It's hard to accept the idea that you might not be destined for extraordinary things. But by the definition of the word, in order for some people to be extraordinary the rest need to be average or below. Even so, "average" has become the new standard of failure. Millions believe that accepting mediocrity is agreeing to a worthless life. However, the people that do become extraordinary do so because they are obsessed with improvement, not because they think they are special.

It's okay to want basic things out of life. At some point, you may learn that the ordinary is all that really matters.

Key Thoughts

"...Entitlement is a failed strategy. It's just another high. It's not happiness."

"The rare people who do become truly exceptional at something do so not because they believe they're exceptional. On the contrary, they become amazing because they're obsessed with improvement. And that

obsession with improvement stems from an unerring belief that they are, in fact, not that great at all."

Chapter 4: The Value of Suffering

Main Idea:

Humans are guilty of dedicating large portions of their lives to entirely useless causes. Whether it's continuing to fight in a war that's already been lost or die in search of mythical creatures, an enormous amount of suffering can be avoided. Yet, if you ask these people if they would have changed their behavior, most would say no. Choosing how you suffer, even if it's altogether pointless, is powerfully fulfilling. You have control over what you will suffer from, so it's important to ask yourself why you are suffering and what the purpose is.

Supporting Ideas:

The Self-Awareness Onion

Just like peeling an onion, pulling back layers of inner life is likely to end in tears. The layers of self-awareness are:

1. Understanding what your emotions are

2. Ability to ask why these emotions exist

3. Understanding the standard by which you judge yourself.

Most people are terrible at understanding themselves. They don't know why they feel disappointed in their successes or why the behavior of relatives is so hurtful. Pulling out the answers to these three questions is deeply painful, but they are full of powerful insight.

Rock Star Problems

Successful people feel like failures when held to the wrong standard. Though Dave Mustaine achieved incredible success as the founder of the Megadeth, he spent his life feeling like a failure because he was once cut from Metallica, one of the greatest rock bands ever. To the outsider, Dave was living the good life, but he wasn't ever able to appreciate it for himself because of the impossible standard he contrasted his successes against.

To change how you feel about your problems, change the standard of comparison. Some metrics are better than others, and many will make you feel terrible no matter what you accomplish. Change the metric and you will soon feel better about yourself.

Shitty Values

People devote great portions of their lives to pursuing things that leave them empty.

- **Pleasure**: Seeking short term pleasure at the cost of long term satisfaction leads to anxiety, emotional instability and depression. Instead of seeing pleasure as the CAUSE of happiness, it's healthier to understand it as an effect of a balanced life.

- **Material Success:** Only a minimal amount of money improves happiness for the better, the rest just acts as a hollow status symbol.

- **Always Being Right:** Brains are terrible at knowing when things are true. It's never a good idea to base your self-worth on being right, because you will inevitably let yourself down.

- **Staying Positive:** Sometimes things are truly terrible, and denying negative emotions leads to avoidance of the problems in front of you.

Defining Good and Bad Values

To live a life with good values, check that they are based in realty, good for society, and both immediate and controllable. In contrast, damaging values will be superstitious, destructive for society, and difficult for you to control. Healthy values can be achieved internally, while destructive ones rely on events beyond your control. By prioritizing your values in healthy ways, you can better influence your daily decision making process to work towards what you truly want.

Key Thoughts

"If suffering is inevitable, if our problems in life are unavoidable, then the question we should be asking is not 'How do I stop suffering?' but 'Why am I suffering—for what purpose?'"

"Our values determine the metrics by which we measure ourselves and everyone else... If you want to change how you see your problems, you should change what you value and/or how you measure failure/success."

"This is why these values—pleasure, material success, always being right, staying positive—are poor ideals for a person's life. Some of the greatest moments of one's life are not pleasant, not successful, not known, and not positive."

Chapter 5: You are Always Choosing

Main Idea:

The difference between being forced to run a marathon and choosing to run one is the amount of training and preparation you go through. The race will still be painful either way, but proper preparation could make it one of the proudest moments of your life. In the same way, choosing the problems you face is empowering, while having problems forced upon makes us feel like victims.

Supporting Ideas:

The Choice

We are all responsible for everything that happens in our lives, and coming to terms with that is a powerful way to remove your personal limitations. It's not possible to control what happens to us, but it's always possible to choose our response, and not controlling our response is just another form of choosing it. There's no way to not care about everything, so the essential question is carefully choosing what to care about.

The Responsibility/Fault Fallacy

Taking responsibility for your life is powerful. If you feel like no one will date you because you are unlovable, you are holding yourself back and not staying open to the lovers that would prove you wrong. 'Fault' and responsibility are two different things. Taking responsibility for the problems in your life doesn't mean you caused them to happen, it means you are willing to take the steps to solve them. Lots of people are likely at fault for your unhappiness, but only you are responsible for moving past it. No one else is responsible for your current situation but you, and accepting that is the first step to moving forward.

Responding to Tragedy

Even intense, horrible events are still your responsibility to deal with. The underlying truth of fault and responsibility doesn't vary based on severity, and the sooner you choose to deal with the ramifications, the better for you.

Genetics and the Hand We're Dealt

Everyone is born with a certain form of disadvantage that makes life harder in certain areas. It's easy to feel powerless against these disadvantages and avoid the blame for them, but the truth is we are still responsible for them. Even poker is more about skill than the cards you're dealt, so the limitations you are born with are your responsibility to accept and overcome. No one else will do it for you.

Victimhood Chic

It's easy to delay accepting responsibility for the direction of your life and play the role of the victim instead. The internet and social media has made it easier than ever to push blame on other parties and publicly shame or blame anything but ourselves for our problems. Not only is this distracting from the real solutions to our problems, it also dilutes victimhood so that the real victims are no longer able to be identified.

There is No "How"

Making a change to accept responsibility isn't supposed to be a difficult transition, it's simply choosing a different choice. At first, you'll feel like a failure and doubt your decision, but over time you will come to see that the necessary, painful side effects of changing what you care about and work towards are entirely worth it for the progress that you're making.

Key Thoughts

"There is a simple realization from which all personal improvement and growth emerges. This is the realization that we, individually, are responsible for everything in our lives, no matter the external circumstances."

Chapter 6: You're Wrong About Everything (But So Am I)

Main Idea:

We're all wrong about almost everything, but few people are willing to admit it. Your beliefs about the world have changed dramatically since childhood, and they'll continue to change as you age. For this reason, it's almost idiotic to be obsessed with being "right", as what feels right is subject to constant flux. In this way, limiting beliefs like 'I'm not smart or attractive' are especially damaging because they hold you back from going after what you want because you assume you know what will happen. Take the chance to prove your beliefs wrong and you might be amazed at the result.

Supporting Ideas:

Architects of Our Own Beliefs

We all think we see patterns in otherwise random events, and our brains are always drawing connections that don't exist. Because the brain is an imperfect tool, it's incapable of always recognizing these faulty patterns, which is why so many of our deepest held beliefs turn out wrong.

Be Careful What You Believe

False memories in the brain are disturbingly common, even when it comes to horrible crimes like incest. Your brain can't be trusted to tell you the whole truth of a situation because it operates as an imperfect pattern-finding machine. People that are unsatisfied with their lives will find it all too easy to jump to a conclusion that fits the pattern in their brain, making it easy to manufacture false beliefs about themselves that hold them back.

The Dangers of Pure Certainty

Absolute certainty about the world can be incredibly dangerous if it's not properly challenged. You can set goals for yourself, visualize them every day, and work towards them with single mindedness, but if you're aiming at the wrong target it's all a complete waste. Criminals often feel good about their crimes because they feel deep down that they were justified. In contrast, an acceptance of uncertainty is where real progress is made.

Manson's Law of Avoidance

(Mark) Manson's law of avoidance states that 'The more something threatens your identity, the more you will avoid it'. Good and bad things alike can challenge what you believe about yourself, making them difficult to pursue. If you're afraid to take a stab at your dream because of a fear of failure, you are feeling threatened enough by the idea of challenging your identity to not go after what you want. Until you overcome the comfort of having a set view of yourself, you won't be able to move towards your dreams.

Kill Yourself

In Buddhism, the idea of being an individual being is a mental construction that holds us all back. Likewise, there are psychological benefits to not approaching life as a separate being because it frees you up to take risks and try new things. The truth is that there is little that is unique or special about your problems, and realizing this makes it easier to work towards change.

How to Be a Little Less Certain of Yourself

To start challenging yourself to doubt your deep-held beliefs, it's important to ask yourself the following questions.

- *What if I'm wrong?* If your views are putting you at odds with almost everyone around you, the problem is probably you, not them.

- *What would it mean if I'm wrong?* Once you admit that you're wrong, are you willing to take the steps to change your behavior?

- *Would being wrong create a better or worse problem than my current problem, for both myself and others?* It's impossible to avoid problems in life, but you can find the insight to decide whether being wrong will create better or worse problems for yourself.

Key Thoughts

"Uncertainty is the root of all progress and all growth. As the adage goes, the man who believes he knows everything learns nothing.

We cannot learn anything without first not knowing something. The more we admit we do not know, the more opportunities we gain to learn."

Chapter 7: Failure Is the Way Forward

Main Idea:

Failure is the Way Forward

Sometimes, failure is one of the best ways to set yourself up for success. Entering the job market during a brutal recession gave Mark the willingness to try starting an online company because he had nothing to lose. That decision led to his long-term success and catapulted his career in previously unthinkable directions. Failure is relative, so allowing yourself the ability to pursue risky dreams because you have nothing to lose can be a way to accomplish more than you can imagine.

Supporting Ideas:

The Failure/Success Paradox

Children learn to walk by falling over and over. In the same way, learning to make beautiful paintings involves hours of creating terrible art first. It's impossible to become good at anything that you're not willing to fail at, and it's also crucial to use metrics for success that rely on you, not any outside factors. So long as the motivation to press forward comes from inside and is less dependent on results, you have the drive necessary to make it a success.

Pain is Part of the Process

Studies of survivors of war often finds that they look back at times of immense hardship as essential for shaping them into better people. Pain is often essential for growth, and the difficult step of starting the process is often the hardest part of all. Even so, painfully jumping into something is the only way to make meaningful progress.

The "Do Something" Principle

No matter what your goals are, the important thing is to start doing something (no matter how small) to make them a reality. Once you start, you will learn as you go, but getting yourself comfortable with the first step is the most important part of all. You aren't supposed to have all the answers or even know what questions to ask, but the process of getting started will help you fill in the blanks over time. Action is necessary for getting the snowball of motivation rolling, and once you start you are likely to find that ideas will flood in for you.

Key Thoughts

"Life is about not knowing and then doing something anyway. All of life is like this. It never changes. Even when you're happy. Even when you're farting fairy dust. Even when you win the lottery and buy a small fleet of Jet Skis, you still won't know what the hell you're doing. Don't ever forget that. And don't ever be afraid of that."

"Don't just sit there. Do something. The answers will follow."

Chapter 8: The Importance of Saying No

Main Idea:

For Mark, years spent traveling the world left him with different ideas of how various cultures care about the way they express themselves. Especially memorable for him was "Russian Frankness", or Eastern European people's ability to give honest answers, even if the truth was mildly offensive. He quickly learned that one culture's way of proper behavior can be completely different and even unacceptable somewhere else. For this reason, it's important to challenge your assumptions about what is normal and be comfortable with alternatives, as millions of people around the world might already accept them.

Supporting Ideas:

Rejection Makes Your Life Better

Western culture has quickly taken to heart the mentality that it's important to be accepting and affirmative to ourselves and everyone we meet. However, rejecting nothing means that you also stand for nothing. Avoiding rejection is considered a way to live a happier life, but in truth it often just makes life meaningless. By rejecting certain career paths, you can fully invest yourself in one and experience the joy that comes with becoming an expert at your job after 30 years of effort. Avoiding rejection, confrontation and conflict makes it impossible to take a stand for what matters, meaning it's important to start training yourself to say the word "no" more often.

Boundaries

The story of Romeo and Juliet is a classic example of what happens when boundaries aren't properly followed. After all, the story is about two teenagers who meet, fall in love and within a week wind up dead. In fact, some people believe Shakespeare wrote the story to satirize romantic love. Unfortunately, many people follow the example of heady, thoughtless love found in Romeo and Juliet and live their lives impulsively, no matter the negative consequences.

In contrast, creating strong boundaries makes it easier to accept that things might not always be perfect with making yourself crazy in the process. Highs and lows are bound to happen in any relationship, but not allowing yourself to be overly committed to the emotional swings is essential.

How to Build Trust

When interacting with his wife before going out on a date, Mark isn't afraid to let her know when she doesn't look her best. This might earn him a smack in the moment, but over the long term it has worked to build up her trust of him and to better believe him when he tells her that she looks amazing. This creates a bond of trust between them that can outlast the momentary insult of being told when her outfit is lacking.

In all relationships, trust is the most important ingredient. A lack of trust is why people get caught having affairs, and why it's never right to believe someone that says an affair "just happened to them". Instead, cheaters need to go through an introspective process to understand what it is in their relationship that is more important to them than their partner. Only by learning what is competing for their attention and willingly giving it up can they work to restore their relationship.

Freedom Through Commitment

While western culture is teaching us that the key to happiness is to surround ourselves with more stuff, the truth is that it's often easier to be happier when you have less. Too many opportunities or decisions can be incredibly stressful, which is why making commitments that produce fewer options in the long run is often better. Likewise, compromising on the number of experiences means you have more chances to go deeply in any one experience. The more time you spend with one job/country/spouse, the deeper and more complex your understanding and appreciation will be for it. While it's important to experience as much as you can while you are young and impressionable, it pays to stay on a track later in life to ensure you experience the joys of what a long-term commitment can bring.

Key Thoughts

"For a relationship to be healthy, both people must be willing and able to both say no and hear no. Without that negation, without that occasional rejection, boundaries break down

and one person's problems and values come to dominate the others."

Chapter 9 ...And Then You Die

Main Idea:

Death can come quickly, and when it does, it disrupts every corner of a settled life. Mark lost a friend in his teens, and the event triggered a depressive cycle in his life that lasted for months. Eventually, however, the death came to mark a turning point for him and became an event that helped him clarify what he wanted from life and understand that there was no time to waste before going after it. In many ways, encounters with death is how we come to rediscover meaning in our lives, and to understand what is truly worth caring about above all else.

Supporting Ideas:

Something Beyond Ourselves

After years of apparent failure, the great author and professor Ernest Becker came to terms with his terminal illness by writing *The Denial of Death,* an influential work on psychology and anthropology. In his book, he outlined the fact that humans are the only creatures that can conceptualize death and can think about alternative versions of what their lives might look like, which gives most humans a "death terror" when they think about their own demise. Second, he argued that all humans have two parts of themselves: a physical and conceptual self.

We are terrified to lose ourselves to death, which is why humans try to build a "legacy" of achievements like discoveries, named buildings and published books. In our minds, this is a way to live on past death and not succumb to the terror of nonexistence. However, Becker believed that these projects were part of the problem, not the solution, for facing death. Rather than live a fruitless existence attempting to create a legacy, it's far better to let go of this fear and chose the values of living freely and without the restraint of seeking immortality in some form.

The Sunny Side of Death

In the same way that Becker believed death shouldn't be feared, approaching death can also be a way to become closer to living. Standing at the edge of a cliff will make you more aware of your own heartbeat, not to mention how quickly everything could end. In the same way, living a life that is comfortable with the idea of death is one of the best ways to ensure you are fully living.

In truth, the only question worth asking about life is whether you leave it having made the world a better place. Life today is full of feelings of entitlement, meaning it's easy to feel like you've earned something even without putting in the effort for it. In the same way, we all need to work to choose what we want to accomplish, so that we can be sure we aren't wasting our time caring about the wrong things. In truth, that is the easiest way to ensure that your life isn't worth living.

Key Thoughts

"Because once we become comfortable with the fact of our own death—the root terror, the underlying anxiety motivating all of life's frivolous ambitions—we can then choose our values more freely, unrestrained by the illogical quest for immortality, and freed from dangerous dogmatic views."

"The pampering of the modern mind has resulted in a population that feels deserving of something without earning that something, a

population that feels they have a right to something without sacrificing for it."

Thank You

Hope you've enjoyed your reading experience!

We here at CompanionReads will always strive to deliver to you the highest quality guides.

So, we'd like to thank you for supporting us and reading until the very end.

Before you go, would you mind leaving us a review on Amazon?

It means a lot to us and supports us in creating high quality guides for you in the future.

Thanks once again and here's where you can leave us a review:

http://bit.ly/1clickreview

Warmly yours,

The CompanionReads Team